21 THINGS I WISH I KNEW PRIOR TO GIVING BIRTH

21 THINGS I WISH I KNEW PRIOR TO GIVING BIRTH

The working woman's pocket guide to maximizing joy and health in late stage pregnancy.

MARSHA JACOBY

Certified Parenting and Fertility Life Coach

Charleston, SC
www.PalmettoPublishing.com

21 Things I Wish I Knew Prior to Giving Birth

First Edition

Paperback ISBN: 978-1-63837-005-5

*This book is designed for all of you very busy "moms to be" who need the quick, no nonsense low down of what's to come in the next chapter of your life! Consider it the beginning of your **Parenting Mindfulness List**....which will offer you enlightenment to help guide you forward on your incredibly blissful, satisfying, challenging, and delightful role of **Mom**.*

I wish you the ENERGY to be present in every joyful moment, the PATIENCE to move gracefully over any bumps in the road, and the TIME to nurture and love your new baby to the fullest.

TABLE OF CONTENTS

INTRODUCTION

As a realist, I choose to approach every situation armed with as much knowledge as I can muster. Somehow, the real "scoop" regarding the transition from pregnancy to motherhood isn't our society's main topic of conversation. It seems to me that the emphasis is placed on the birthing process, and dialogue regarding all the "tools" and material goods necessary to welcome our babies take precedence. Interestingly, the most critical issues regarding this transition are somehow divorced from conversations, leaving new moms a bit baffled and certainly overwhelmed about a host of issues. I once heard a woman describe the chapter in her life as a new mom as one in which she felt as if someone had thrown a blanket over her, leaving me to further ponder the whirlwind new moms are caught up in given their new role as caretaker to an infant. There is no instruction manual given, yet what we all want is to provide the best care possible for our precious babies. Being a mother is life's greatest honor and privilege.

Breastfeeding and CPR Instruction is exceedingly important, however, there are many topics that should have **equal coverage** and weight in your transition to motherhood. In my estimation, there are 21 issues to consider, ponder and research before, during and after your babies blessed birth. I pray you'll find this listing useful in preparing for the greatest adventure of your life: PARENTHOOD.

Please note: my intention in asking you to review and be mindful of these issues is to allow you to then put them aside at some point (as best you can) and be PRESENT/"in the moment" with your little angel via as many precious moments as possible. We - and you - will never pass this way again! Delight in the wonder and miracle of your newborn.

With Gratitude,

Marsha

#1

SPEAK UP AND ASK!

As a nurse once told me, when you enter the hospital you leave your "dignity at the door". My intention is not to scare you of course, however, the dressing gown and pending birthing process leaves us somewhat bare and vulnerable. Prior to entering this zone, put your mind in gear and remind yourself to be "your own advocate". Bring your voice to the hospital and:

- If you're experiencing pain....ask for pain meds.

- If you're itchy.....ask for anti-itch cream, or meds for this.

- If you're wet....ask for pads or to be changed.

- If your room mate has visitors late in the evening or too late for you, ask that they be kicked out!

- If you're about to have an epidural, and a new resident is going to make the attempt....ask for someone more experienced!

Most nurses will be happy to strive to satisfy you, at least the good ones will. If you don't get satisfaction..... ask a different person (perhaps someone from the next shift). Make your time as comfortable as possible; YOU DESERVE IT!! Also, make an attempt to get sufficient rest; you will need it!

#2

KNOW THAT LAMAZE INSTRUCTORS ARE WONDERFUL, ALBEIT NOT ALWAYS RIGHT

I highly recommend Lamaze Classes as they will bond you and your partner as a couple and make your spouse/partner an integral part of the birthing process. The breathing exercises learned during these sessions will prove valuable in numerous instances eg. during contractions as well as during birth. Many instructors however will tell you that "your body will do what it's supposed to do"... which is not always true. In my case, I never dilated! Well, I did dilate, but only one centimeter. The inherent message here: be prepared for the unexpected and trust modern medicine. If your baby is not delivered *naturally,* does it truly make a difference? Is it worth pursuing a natural, vaginal delivery if there's a risk for you or your unborn child?

Just some questions to ponder.....there is no right or wrong, unless your health or that of your baby is at risk.

#3

WHETHER YOU'RE PLANNING
TO BREAST FEED OR NOT,
YOU SHOULD KNOW
THE BENEFITS....

So that you can make an educated decision for you and your baby. The reason why breastfeeding is so critical after birth is so that your baby can benefit from the colostrum you produce which is considered SUPERFOOD for your newborn. Within minutes of your baby being born you can begin to breastfeed!

COLOSTRUM WILL DO SIX THINGS:

1. help your baby build a strong immune system

2. create a tough coating on your baby's stomach to keep germs from causing illness

3. act as a laxative to allow your baby to pass meconium (the first dark poop)

4. help prevent jaundice

5. give your baby's brain, eyes and heart the right blend of nutrients to grow

6. provide high levels of protein, fat and vitamins for complete nutrition.

Hopefully, if you make the decision to breast feed, you will do so without any issue. If there is an issue however, there are lactation consultants at the hospital who can assist you and your baby and offer guidance. My advice: find out who this person is PRIOR to entering the hospital! Have your partner/spouse/

friend call right after you deliver for an appointment! Have this specialist observe and offer tips for proper positioning and guidance.

If in fact you've had a C-section, it may take a few days for your milk supply to come in. In this case, if your baby is not satisfied, you can consider supplementing with a few ounces of formula. As my British baby nurse said, sometimes you need to "top them off". Remember: BABIES SLEEP WHEN THEIR BELLIES ARE FULL! Don't feel guilty about adding formula to the mix; you're feeding your baby and allowing them much needed rest!

PLEASE NOTE THESE TWO
IMPORTANT POINTS:

1. If, for ANY reason - physical or otherwise, you make the decision NOT to breastfeed (the decision is sometimes made for you by your body), try to STAVE OFF the guilt you might feel and instead replace those sentiments with all of the POSITIVE thoughts and emotions you can muster. This experience may be THE

MOST special of your lifetime; please do not let an inability or lack of desire to breastfeed ruin one moment!!

2. In the case in which breastfeeding is not possible for you but you still have a desire to give your baby the nutrients that breast milk provides, there's a very new option you may wish to consider called BIOMILQ. This is a new scientific process where in a laboratory, human mammary epithelial cells (you can use your own) are utilized to produce human breast milk. (See www.biomilq.com for further information).

#4

LEARN HOW TO PUMP!

KEY FACT: The more you breast feed your baby and the more you pump, the more of a supply you will have!

Even if breastfeeding comes naturally for you, learn how to pump breast milk. Why? Because you don't want to be the ONLY person who has the ability to feed your baby.

PUMPING WILL DO THESE
IMPORTANT THINGS FOR YOU:

- enable you to sleep for a few hours while your spouse/partner feeds your baby

- allow your spouse/partner to share the blessed bonding time that you, the mother, are experiencing....and everyone else is craving!

- enable you to build your milk supply (the more you pump, the more you have!)

- give you the ability to MEASURE how much your baby is drinking which will ease your concerns if you feel you're not producing enough, OR if you're concerned that your baby isn't drinking enough/gaining enough weight.

FIND OUT: If your hospital will allow you to RENT a pump (often theirs are hospital grade and may be stronger than the ones you might buy at a retail store).

Let's move on to the post partum period.....

#5

BODILY CHANGES

After birth, it's natural to feel quite swollen, and I was surprised and dismayed by the fact that I still looked and felt pregnant AFTER having given birth! NO FAIR! In my mind, my body was supposed to go back to the way it was BEFORE.....yet the excess weight was still there! NO ONE TOLD ME THIS WOULD BE THE CASE, and it can be depressing, but take heart! Breastfeeding does take significant weight off! It won't happen overnight....and you shouldn't even be concerned as the priority is a healthy diet to support you and your newborn (if you are breastfeeding). Assuming you are, your food intake is critical at this point as your baby's brain and nervous system are developing. Be sure to make the healthiest choices such as:

- fish, which has DHA, and contains an omega 3 fatty acid which will assist in brain and nervous system development

- milk and yogurt - to provide you with adequate calcium to support bone health

- protein and fiber (eg. lean meat, poultry and whole grains) - which will make you feel full and provide you with energy!

Take heart in the fact that over the course of your baby's first year, with proper nutrition and enough strolling, you should lose 1-2 pounds per week. Think about it this way... it took you nine months to get to this point....it will probably warrant the same amount of time to take it off!

#6

KNOW ABOUT SLEEP TRAINING PRIOR TO GIVING BIRTH!

People don't think you "sleep train" an infant, however you'll learn that everything you do with your baby and/or toddler sets an expectation as you are creating patters of behavior.

As my baby nurse taught me, once your baby is approximately two months old, set him/her down in their bassinet every night between 7 and 8pm. Get them accustomed to being there, and keep this pattern consistent for as many years as possible!

This practice will give you a much deserved evening to yourself! It will also give your child a terrific start. A well rested child is a happy child, and a happy child is a well behaved child.

A key book to read on this topic is *Healthy Sleep, Happy Child* by Dr. Mark Weissbluth, who studied sleep habits in children for over thirty years.

#7

THINK ABOUT WHAT YOU'LL FEED YOUR CHILD ONCE THEY BEGIN TO EAT SOLIDS

THE SIX MONTH POINT...

I bring this up because I want you to know that most foods are acceptable in very tiny quantities, however, it is beneficial to start thinking about how you'll feed your baby so that you're prepared in advance. Will you steam vegetables? Bake potatoes? We want to offer our babies the most nutritious foods available....and start them off on the right path, thus forethought is key here. If you're not a cook, start thinking through your options and read about easy ways to feed your child; at least gather books you can peruse during your baby's first few months. Ask your friends and family members; you'll surely find a wealth of information here!

#8

BABY PROOF YOUR MARRIAGE!

Suggestion: Read an article or two each day about current events in an effort to have ADULT conversation with your partner.

Let's face it....your baby will be the most adorable creature on the planet but....even though you're exhausted, you still need to have adult time! No one can expect you to read the newspaper cover to cover but for the sake of your marriage/partnership and "good talk time with your partner" try to read one or two articles each day so that you can connect on a topic OUTSIDE of your baby. This will serve to keep your conversation fresh, interesting and stimulating! It will also keep you "grounded" as a couple.

#9

SEEK OUT AT LEAST ONE IN-PERSON NEW MOM'S GROUP TO JOIN

It's so important and therapeutic to connect with women going through the same experience as you. These moms are the people you may feel very bonded with over time. They will laugh and cry with you. They will empathize with you, and serve as your cheerleader and companion. You will coach EACH OTHER! The friends you make when your children are babies often become lifelong friends. You are connecting during a very critical and exciting time in your life as you enter your parenthood journey....it's the "birds of a feather" story!

#10

TAKE ALL THE INPUT/ RECOMMENDATIONS YOU RECEIVE WITH A *"GRAIN OF SALT"* AND FOLLOW YOUR GUT!

Once you give birth (and even before), it may feel as if everyone has a suggestion or piece of advice to offer....hopefully no criticism. Be prepared to respond...whether you like it or not you can say "thanks for the suggestion" and move forward doing what YOU believe to be appropriate. Stick with your GUT INSTINCT, and DISMISS all negativity! There's too much to enjoy right now to be pulled off track! Please remember, the people around you mean well and are anxious to reminisce and tell you "their story" and experiences. Be polite...and proceed as you choose.

#11

LEARN HOW TO USE A BABY BJORN AND ENJOY THE WORLD HANDS FREE!

By the time I discovered how to use my baby bjorn, my son was thirteen pounds and too heavy for me to carry around on my chest. However, the last time I did make the attempt, I was at a crowded holiday party and it allowed me to mingle and feel very liberated! Start early and enjoy the special closeness that allows you to bond while going about your chores, daily activities and errands (especially if you're in a walkable community).

There are many different versions; you don't need to spend a fortune (check out Target). Avoid the baby bjorns that require two people to "suit up" and opt for the ones you can administer alone.

Moms aren't the only ones who adore the closeness these allow you to experience. Fathers love these as well as they allow you and baby to explore the world together!

#12

KNOW THAT YOUR CREW OF
FRIENDS MAY SHIFT AND
REGROUP FOR A WHILE....

You're about to embark on an amazing journey, and the outpouring of love you'll feel from friends, family and coworkers will surely be touching. That said, there may be a few in your the crowd, perhaps with fertility issues, who want to be there for you but cannot because of their own pain. These friends surely deserve your empathy, and may not be able to partake in the joyous cloud that surrounds you right now. Hopefully, in time...that changes.

You'll also be making new friends given your new found status, and that's all good! Your focus in life will change from what it was before. You might be dining in vs. dining out and passing on late night TV which you might have relished before....all small sacrifices for the scintillating moments you'll have with your little one!

#13

FEEL FREE TO CALL THE PEDIATRICIAN AS OFTEN AS YOU LIKE WITH QUESTIONS AND/OR CONCERNS

Don't feel as if you have to wait for an appointment! Nothing is more of a priority than the health and comfort of your baby. In addition, remind yourself that your doctor WANTS to field your call. If you believe that's not the case however, and are concerned that you'll be viewed as an annoyance, find another pediatrician! So....if your baby's skin tone looks yellow....call! If you feel your baby is not eating enough....call! If you're concerned that your baby is not sleeping enough.....call!

It's critical for you to have PEACE OF MIND so that YOU can sleep and take care of yourself. Don't hesitate.....make that call your priority!

#14

CONSIDER THE KEY FACTS ABOUT CARETAKERS, NANNIES, AND BABY NURSES

If you will be hiring a babysitter, nanny or baby nurse, you want to know about them and their prior experiences as well as possible BEFORE they begin. You are entrusting that individual with the most precious element in your life: your child! There are many interview questions on the internet; take advantage of this wealth of information and study up! Attempt to ask the questions that will give you the most valuable insight and start outlining your interview.

For a caretaker of a newborn, my preference would be to hire a woman who has had her own children, as this ensures terrific experience. References are key, and mothers will spend significant amounts of time on the phone discussing their caretaker experiences in huge detail so ask these references when they will have time to speak and book an "appointment to talk"; it's important that you learn everything you can about this candidate. In my experience, mother's will be honest....and tell you if there were any "red flags" or incidents that made them uncomfortable. Explore and think through these considerably; your gut will tell you if you should move forward or move on toward a new candidate.

Once you hire a caretaker, keep in mind that this is NOT the person that needs to remain in place forever! The duration for a baby nurse is normally 6-8 weeks, and she'll typically tell you that she's booked for another assignment at that time. Keep in mind.... if you're not feeling comfortable about the person you chose (again, go with your gut), interview again and find someone new! There are extremely qualified people out there in need of employment. ASK, ASK, ASK local moms for references and reach out on your local Facebook page as every town and city has a site for parents where this information will be responded to within thirty seconds! So look on Manhattan Moms, Great Neck Moms, Tenafly Moms....you'll find a wealth of valuable information from other moms who are empathetic and eager to help!

That said, OBSERVE BEFORE HIRING: Pay your candidates for 60-90 minutes of assistance while you're also home, and make yourself scarce. Pretend to be busy but listen closely....and watch from the corner of your eye. Is this person "connecting" with your baby? Does she seem like a natural? Are you comfortable with the way she's holding her/him? Is she talking/singing to your baby? Is she someone who could teach YOU proper holding and bathing techniques? If she does leave the house with baby, do a "drive by". Is she answering her phone very often? Is she chatting with baby while they sit in the park? You'll get a gut feeling quickly, and your baby will tell you what he/she thinks as well. If she's too fussy or unhappy, she's letting you know that this is NOT the right person.

As infants, my twins had a baby nurse. My boys always love experiences that involve water (even from birth). Whenever our first nurse bathed them, they each screamed and fussed terribly, which pained me to hear. I learned over the first few weeks that this woman was not competent....but should have known earlier from the cries of my boys. We must listen to their cues as these precious newbies are talking to us and communicating the only way they can.

#15

BOND AND FOSTER
BRAIN DEVELOPMENT;
SING AND TALK TO YOUR
BABY CONSTANTLY!

Researchers note that your baby can identify your voice as early as 24-27 weeks in utero. No matter how you think you sound, they love hearing your voice.... even prior to making an appearance on Planet Earth!

At birth, your baby's brain contains 100 billion neurons. During his or her first years, he will grow trillions of brain cell connections called neural synapses. When you provide loving, language enriched experiences for your baby, you are giving his neural connections and pathways more opportunities to become wired together.

There was a study done at the University of Kansas (Hart, Risley, 1995) that concluded that the greater the number of words children heard from their parents and/or caregivers PRIOR to age three, the higher their IQ and academic performance was!

Talk and sing as often as possible! Calming, rhythmic melodies help children to remember, and cements information in their brains! So brush up, and learn as many baby songs as you can; consider Old MacDonald, Row, Row, Row Your Boat and the ABC song. 85% of a child's brain develops in the first three years of life, so place as much information in as possible within that window of opportunity! You will surely reap the benefits of your diligent efforts!

Repetition and familiarity is comforting for your baby, and that is what fosters the development of language, so be prepared to sing the same songs and read the same books over and over and over. Your precious baby will love it!

#16

PREVENT SUDDEN INFANT DEATH SYNDROME (SIDS)

When putting your angel to bed, it's critical to place your baby flat on his/her back whether it's daytime OR nighttime. Stomach and side sleeping is not appropriate for an infant. Please do NOT place a blanket, quilt, or stuffed animal in the crib, and ensure that every caretaker is aware of this and the reasons why an empty crib is perfect! SIDS is sadly, the number one cause of death in children from ages one month to one year (Nemours Foundation, 2017).

Once your baby can roll over on his/her own (approximately 6 months) they can choose their own sleep position.

STUDIES SHOW THAT MANY FACTORS LOWER THE INCIDENCE OF SIDS:

- Breastfeeding - breast milk prevents infections that may lead to SIDS

- Having a baby sleep in the same room as his/her mother

- Putting a baby to sleep with a pacifier (only do this after one month as earlier may cause nipple confusion)

#17

PRACTICE STRESS REDUCTION TECHNIQUES: DEEP BREATHING, MINDFULNESS, VISUALIZATION, AND MEDITATION

While pregnant, during childbirth and after giving birth, these techniques can calm your mind and body and allow you stolen moments you will come to relish. Your pace and sleep schedule will change dramatically, thus the following strategies are an essential part of your "parenting tool kit." It's a good idea to start practicing these now....

- **Deep Breathing** (also known as belly breathing)

  This technique can lower your blood pressure and allow your body to relax.

  Breathe in through your nose, fill up your diaphragm with air and feel it extend, hold for a second or two and slowly breath out through your mouth. Do this exercise for five minutes and build to twenty if you're feeling anxious.

- **Visualization** - Imagine that the air you're breathing in is full of light and calmness, and that as you're releasing your breath, you're ridding your body of toxins.

- **Mindfulness** (taking the time to "smell the roses"). Mindfulness is key as we're all so preoccupied and are multitasking to the max. Practicing mindfulness will assure you that you won't miss the special moments that you'll want to look back and dwell upon forty years from now!

- **Meditation** - You can do this quietly, on your own, or with the assistance of an app on your phone (such as the Calm app) which will offer you narrated sessions where you can choose the amount of time.

Being a parent means taking a STEP BACK, slowing down your pace, and enjoying the moment. If you can utilize these methods and incorporate them in your life ongoingly, you will end up healthier, and those around you (especially your child) will reap the benefits of your serene demeanor.

#18

LEARN HOW TO BATHE YOUR INFANT

I pray you're blessed to have an amazing nurse at the hospital who can take the time to demonstrate the correct way to bathe an infant. If not, no worries, as there are many Youtube videos that can illustrate this process well.

Please ponder this time through beforehand however, and take it very seriously! A mental "Do Not Disturb" sign is in order here. When bathing your newborn, please keep baby SAFE:

- DO NOT answer your phone

- Avoid looking at text messages

- Let your spouse/partner know that you will be bathing baby

- Have all items laid out in advance

- NEVER leave your baby

- Test water temperature beforehand

Purchase an infant tub with a soft insert now so that you have it ready on time. There are people that will tell you to bathe your baby in the sink; that never felt right to me.

Most babies enjoy water, and bath time for an infant should be soothing and offer special bonding time. Be "present " and cherish this time together.

#19

HAVE YOUR "TO DO LISTS"
READY AND CHECK OFF ITEMS
PRIOR TO DELIVERING!

BELOW ARE SAMPLE LISTS
TO GET YOU STARTED:

FOR BABY:

- Infant bathtub with soft insert

- Bassinet with mattress pad and sheets

- Bottles (even if your goal is to breast feed this allows another person to feed breast milk. Boil these in advance so they're sanitized and ready to go!)

- Pacifiers (boil these in advance so they're sanitized and ready to go!)

- Clothes for baby including a sleeper for nighttime (a sleeping gown that zips; especially beneficial in cold temperatures as some are made in a heavy fabric)

- Diapers and Diaper Garbage Pail (to eliminate odor from your house)

- Infant Car Seat

- Carriage

FOR YOU:

- Nursing Pillow for breastfeeding - which will serve to prop baby up, diminishing the need for your arms to do all the work, and taking pressure off of your back

- Flip flops for hospital (dispose these upon leaving the hospital; please don't take home any germs!)

- New Nightgowns for hospital (people will pop in unexpectedly; some will take photos)

- Phone and Charger

- Sanitary pads (although they should have these at the hospital to give you)

- Nail File/Makeup/Deoderant (if you like)

- Healthy Snacks/Energy bars - Breastfeeding makes us extremely hungry at all hours!

- Prepare this bag weeks in advance as you never know exactly when your time will come!

#20

KNOW THAT YOUR BABY WILL BE BORN WITH A PERSONALITY. HE/SHE WILL HAVE LIKES AND DISLIKES JUST LIKE YOU!

Each child is born pre-programmed with their own innate personality. One of our many jobs as a parent is to discover their likes and dislikes. When my oldest son was approximately three months old, I came home from work to see my baby napping in his carriage. Under his face which was on its side, was a clean, folded burp cloth. I asked my sitter why it was placed there and her response was "he likes to sleep that way". That's when it struck me; she had gotten acquainted with my son's like and dislikes when he was just an in-fant. Many like to be held a specific way, massaged in a specific way and fed in a specific way. Part of our job as parent is to be "in tune" with our children. That de-notes true closeness, and also sets the stage for a peace-ful existence.

#21

LET GO OF NEGATIVITY AND ENJOY EVERY MOMENT!!

You will never be able to "redo" this time in your life. Savor each moment of your pregnancy and the joy of creation!! Filter out the noise (from other people), prepare in advance (mentally) and care for your physical being each day. Keep yourself on a positive track! You are about to take the ride of your life, so enjoy it to the fullest extent possible. Let others pamper you and ask for assistance when you need it. Surround yourself with individuals who offer you an emotional lift and distance yourself from anyone who might detract from the natural high you might feel. Ask your questions and say your prayers (if that feels right). This is *your* journey; make it one you will always treasure. Believe in yourself. I can tell by the fact that you just completed this book that you're destined to be a wonderful, caring and nurturing mother!!!

BIOGRAPHY

Marsha Jacoby is a Certified Life Coach who has lectured in Long Island on many different topics including *Best Practices for Hiring Caretakers, Healthy Sleep Habits, Developing Academic Excellence via Creative Play, Assisting Fussy Eaters* and *Navigating Technology and Teaching Children to Exist "Unplugged"*. In her one-on-one coaching practice, Marsha helps women to transition into their parenting roles with ease, fostering optimal work/life balance with a focus on new priorities. She resides in Long Island, NY with her husband and three sons. Her own three and a half year fertility journey and parenting experience makes her coaching of these topics very natural.

Marsha also spent over twenty years in financial services, during which time she had a successful and rewarding career in marketing and sales. Her most recent position was Northeast Regional Director at Nationwide Financial Services, where she spent seven years.

Read more about Marsha on her web site: *womenmakingprogress.com,* and view her posts on Face Book at *Fertility Mama Life Coach.*

Copyright April, 2020.

* 9 7 8 1 6 3 8 3 7 0 0 5 5 *